KICK UP SOME GOOD EATS

A Tae Kwon Do Master Instructor's
Recipes For Health
BY: Sixth Degree Black
JIM DUNBAR

MasterDunbar.OceanTKD.com

Copyright 2016 by JAMES DUNBAR

ISBN – 13: 978-1530191222
ISBN – 10: 153019122X

I have had the privilege of knowing Master James Dunbar for many years. His love for people and his quest for excellence is apparent in everything he does. I am anxiously awaiting the release of his cookbook.

Grandmaster Brenda J Sell
U.S. Chung Kwon Do Association

Master Dunbar has been a fountain of information and training for a number of years. I thank him for all of his dedication to the art and life.

Angelo G. Longo, 2nd Dan candidate Ocean Tae Kwon Do and Kukkiwon

TO:

My Grandmasters and all my students of Tae Kwon Do for over the past 30 years.

And Second Degree Black Belt candidate Angelo G. Longo for his invaluable help in formatting this book. As the saying goes, "Sometimes the Student becomes the Teacher".

TABLE OF CONTENTS

PREFACE

It may be noted that I am not a chef, Doctor, dietitian, phycologist or yogi.
I am a 72 year old, Sixth Degree Black Belt Master Instructor of Tae Kwon Do and a member of the United States Chung Do Kwon Association. I have seriously been training and teaching for over the past 35 years.

The word training will be used throughout this book, in reference to Tae Kwon Do, martial art training in general, health and diet.

A little more about myself. A cancer survivor of over thirteen years with on third of my large intestine removed (now I can eat and drink more and get rid of it quicker – not recommended though). Right hip replaced four years ago and was back training within six weeks, and still kicking. As to my bionic hip, wouldn't know I had one, if I wasn't there.

The motivation for writing this book is the sincere hope that it will help the reader to become aware of themselves and work towards a healthier diet, with some form of exercise with fasting and meditation thrown in. All are needed for the fullness of life.

Some of these recipes may not seem tasty or just not to one's liking, that's ok. Use the ones you do like. This is not a health book per say, but it has been found that these recipes work for me and hopefully you will find what works for you.

Recently a sixty year old friend and fellow Tae Kwon do Grandmaster instructor asked me when I was going to retire from training. Being a little shocked, I shocked him back and said "never". I really can't envision not training. Sure, I know my techniques are on the down side of the clime but I am still on the mountain and it is great. As Qua Jang Ed Sell always said "feeling great and getting better every day".

"STAY VERTICAL AND KEEP VENTILATING – MY FRIEND"

The trick is finding what works for you and keep doing it. Please see the references for some great books on diet and life styles.

FASTING: I find it very helpful to try and fast one day per week, before starting my three day diet (see page   ). Some may not be able to fast because of some medical problem and should consult the physician before fasting. There will be more on fasting and meditation in a forth coming book that I am working on.

As the great French Chef Julia Child said "bon appetite"

THREE DAY DIET

Day 1

Breakfast: One-half grapefruit, 2 Tb peanut butter 1 slice dry toast, coffee or tea

Lunch: One half cup dry tuna, 1 slice dry toast, coffee or tea

Dinner: 3 ounces of any meat, 1 cup green beans, 1 cup red beets

1 small apple, ½ cup vanilla ice cream

Day 2

Breakfast: 1 egg, 1 slice dry toast, ½ banana, coffee or tea

Lunch: 1 cup cottage cheese, 5 saltines, coffee or tea

Dinner: 2 hot dogs, 1 cup broccoli, ½ cup carrots, 1 banana, ½ cup vanilla ice cream, coffee or tea

Day 3

Breakfast: 5 saltines, 1 slice cheddar cheese, 1 small apple, Coffee or tea

Lunch: 1 hard boiled egg, 1 slice dry toast, coffee or tea

Dinner: 1 cup dry tuna, 1 cup red beets, 1 cup cauliflower, ½ cantaloupe, ½ cup vanilla ice cream, coffee or tea.

The diet works out to be about 1,000 to 1,100 calories per day. Good to follow every week. You will be surprised to find that you will probably loose about ten pounds

As with any diet one should check with their medical advisor.

APPETIZERS & SNACKS

PEACH CRISP

4 ½ cups peaches
½ cup sugar
2 Tb all-purpose flour
1/8 tsp nutmeg; ¼ tsp cinnamon
Coconut oil
1 cup rolled oats
½ cup brown sugar
¾ cup all-purpose flour
½ tsp salt
¼ cup butter – melted

Mix first 4 ingredients in large bowl, let stand while heating oven to 400 degrees. Coat 9x13 inch baking dish with coconut oil – spoon fruit mixture in dish. Bake for 35 minutes, until bubbly.
Combine oats and next 3 ingredients, drizzle butter over and mix to crumbly. Sprinkle over fruit mixture. Bake another 15 minutes.
Cool – ENJOY.

"EVERYTHING HAS BEAUTY, BUT NOT EVERYONE SEES IT" Confucius

SPINACH NUGGETS

2 10 ounces frozen spinach
1 Tb dried onion
2 cups grated parmesan cheese
2 beaten eggs
3 Tb melted butter
Little cayenne to taste

Cook spinach and onion according to package, drain well. Combine first 4 ingredients then stir in beaten eggs and butter. Form into 1 inch balls and freeze on cookie sheet, then freeze in bags if desired. To serve bake 375 for 15 to 20 minutes or microwave 3-4 minutes on high.

WE ARE WHAT WE EAT

PEANUT BUTTER RICE SNACK

1 cup peanut butter
2 cups rice krispies
2 cups mini marshmallows
2 cups white chocolate chips

Melt peanut butter, chocolate chips and a few
marshmallows in microwave, about 2 minutes.
Mix all together.   YUM

*"Success depends upon previous preparation,
and without such preparation there is sure to
be failure."*
Confucius

DRUNKEN HOT DOGS

1 pound hot dogs
¾ cup bourbon
½ cup brown sugar
¼ cup maple syrup
1 ½ cups ketchup
1 Tb chopped onion
Dash cayenne

Cut hot dogs into bite size pieces. Combine all ingredients. Put into pot or slow cooker bring to boil turn down temperature simmer for one hour. Serve with toothpicks.

THE TRUE SIGN OF INTELLIGENCE IS NOT KNOWLEDGE BUT IMAGINATION.

Liverwurst Spread

½ POUND LIVERWURST
1 Tb sweet relish
¼ cup mayonnaise
1 Tb ketchup
1 tsp prepared mustard
¼ cup minced onion
Dash Worcestershire sauce

Mash liverwurst with fork, mix in rest of
ingredients.
Chill couple of hours.

*FREEDOM IS NOT WORTH HAVING IF IT DOES
NOT
INCLUDE THE FREEDOM TO MAKE MISTAKES*

SEA LEGS DIP

3 pounds sea legs
8 ounces softened cream cheese
3 stalks celery minced
½ cup mayonnaise
    <u>Cocktail Sauce:</u>
1 cup ketchup
1 Tb horseradish
Couple drops lime juice
Couple drops Tabasco Sauce
Dash Old Bay Seasoning

Shred sea legs. Mix in other three ingredients and put into serving bowl. Prepare cocktail sauce, spread over top of sea legs.

IF YOU WANT TO STAND OUT, DON'T BE DIFFERENT; BE OUTSTANDING

White Fish Dip Or Salad

1 pound any white fish
2-3 Tb minced onion
¼ tsp white pepper
Salt to taste
½ cup mayonnaise
'

Cover fish with *water* and bring to lite boil,
lower temperature and cook for five minutes
or until fish starts to fall apart. Drain water and
cool fish down, mix all ingredients, and adjust
mayonnaise to your liking. Cool in refrigerator
for an hour or two. Use as dip or salad.

*INITIAL CHANGE IS DIFFICULT
BUT OFTEN ESSENTIAL TO SURVIVAL*

Tuna Pate

1 8 ounce package cream cheese softened
2 Tb chili sauce
1 Tb dry parsley
1 tsp minced onion
Few dash's Tabasco Sauce
2 cans tuna, drained (6 ½ -7oz cans)

Beet all ingredients until blended.
Cool in refrigerator for a few hours.

*LIFE IS TEN PERCENT WHAT HAPPENS TO YOU
AND NINETY PERCENT HOW YOU RESPOND TO
IT.*

BASIL PESTO

¼ extra virgin olive oil
5 cloves garlic minced
2 cups fresh basil chopped or ½ cup dry
½ cup pine nuts
¼ cup lemon juice or apple cider vinegar
1 tsp sea salt

Put all ingredients in blender and blend. Serve with crackers of choice and or Italian or France bread

BOLDNESS HAS GENIUS, POWER AND MAGIC IN IT.

ARTICHOKE DIP

14 ounce can artichokes hearts, packed in
water, drain
5 ounces feta cheese
½ cup plain or vanilla yogurt
1 scallion minced
2 tsp garlic minced
2 tsp lemon juice or apple cider vinegar
Sea salt and pepper to taste
Sprinkle paprika

Put artichokes, cheese, yogurt and lemon juice
in food processor, pulse a couple of times. Stir
in garlic, salt, pepper and scallion, put in
serving bowl. Sprinkle paprika over top.

OUR ATTITUDE TOWARDS LIFE DETERMINES
LIFE'S ATTITUDE TOWARDS US.

Stuffed Celery

1 bunch celery stalks
Peanut butter
Almond butter
Cream cheese
Seasoned cream cheese

Cut celery stalks into 2-3 inch pieces and fill
each with any of the above fillings.

LIFE CAN BE FUN, DON'T COMPLICATE IT

PEAR CRISP

8 pears, cored and sliced
2 Tb lemon juice
1 tsp grated lemon rind
1 tsp ground ginger
½ cup sugar
4Tb flour
TOPPING: ½ cup brown sugar / 5 Tb whole-wheat flour
¾ rolled oats 4 Tb powdered skim milk;
1 tsp cinnamon; 2 Tb butter

Toss first 4 ingredients together, mix sugar and flour
Sprinkle over pear mixture, spoon into buttered baking
Dish. Mix next 5 ingredients, cut in butter to form fine crumbs
Sprinkle over pear mixture. BAKE 375 degrees
For 30 to 45 minutes.

CHEESE CHIPS

Tired of potato chips? Try these.

Slice about 1/8 thick cheese – sharp; mild;
Swiss; etc.
Fry till firm on very lightly coated olive oiled or
coconut oiled frying pan.

ENJOY

"EDUCATION BREEDS CONFIDENCE."

Confucius

YOGURT BANANA BREAD

1 ¼ cup sugar; ½ cup butter softened
2 large eggs; 3-4 bananas
½ cup yogurt; ¾ cup milk; 1 tsp. vanilla
2 ½ cups all-purpose flour; 1 tsp. baking soda
1 tsp. salt
1 cup chopped nuts and ½+cup raisins
Put oven rack to low position so tops of loaf
pans are in middle. Heat oven to 350 degrees.
Grease 2 loaf pans
8 ½ x 4 ½ x 2 ½.

Blend sugar and butter, blend in eggs well.
Blend in bananas, yogurt, milk, vanilla until
smooth. Mix flour, baking soda and salt – stir
into other ingredients until moistened (don't
over mix). Stir in nuts and raisins.
Bake 1 hour, until toothpick, inserted in
middle, comes out clean.

RAVE REVIEWS

Guacamole Dip

3 large ripe avocados
¼ cup lemon juice
3 cloves garlic
½ small onion finely chopped
1 small tomato chopped
Sea Salt to taste

Place avocados; lemon juice; garlic and salt in
food processor, blend till smooth. Mix in
tomato and onion. Chill

*A CLOUDY DAY IS NO MATCH FOR A SUNNY
DISPOSITION.*

HUMMUS WITH TAHINI

1 can chickpeas (garbanzo)
3 Tb sesame tahini
2 Tb yogurt
1 Tb olive oil
2 cloves garlic minced
¼ tsp. sea salt
Dash cayenne and or cumin
3 Tb lemon juice
1 Tb water
¼ tsp dry parsley or ½ tsp fresh parsley

Drain and rinse chickpeas. Process all in food
processor
Process until smooth. Chill before serving.

YOU ARE WHAT YOU EAT.

PEANUT BUTTER HUMMUS

1 can chickpeas drained and rinse
6 Tb water
¼ cup smooth peanut butter
2 Tb lemon juice
1 clove garlic minced
Salt to taste

Various vegies and chips, to dip.

Process all and chill before serving.

"FOOD ALONE CURES MOST DISEASES."
Hu-Sei-Hui

DEVILED EGGS WITH CRAB

6 hard cooked eggs
3 Tb mayonnaise or yogurt
½ tsp ground mustard
¼+ cup crab meat
1/8 tsp salt
1/8 tsp pepper
Pinch cayenne

Peel eggs, cut lengthwise in half, save white half. Mix yolks with all other Ingredients. Stuff back into white halves.

Alternatives: replace with finely chopped crabmeat, shredded cheese, chopped olives or horseradish crab

ACCEPT CHALLENGES, SO THAT YOU MAY FEEL THE EXHILARATION OF VICTORY.

Turkey Mini Meatballs

1-pound ground turkey (if you insist hamburger)
½ cup dry bread crumbs (panko, plain or seasoned)
¼ cup milk
½ tsp salt
½ tsp Worcestershire sauce
¼ tsp black pepper
1 small onion chopped (1/4 cup)
1 large egg

Mix all ingredients. Shape into 1 inch balls or larger if you want. Place balls in greased pan. Bake 400 degrees 15 to 25 minutes.

"EDUCATION BREEDS CONFIDENCE." - Confucius

BLACK BEAN DIP

1 can (15 ounce) black beans drained
¼ onion diced
1 Tb vegetable broth
½ tsp ground cumin
2 Tb tahini
2 cloves garlic, minced
2 Tb lemon juice
Salt, pepper, cayenne to taste

Process all in food processor. Cool for a couple of hours.
ENJOY

"Not by age but by capacity is wisdom acquired."
Titus Maccius Plautus

BLUE CHEESE DIP

8 ounces' sour cream
8 ounces' mayonnaise or yogurt
3 packages crumbled blue cheese
¼ onion minced
Pinch salt and white pepper

Mix all together cool for hour or two.
This is very similar to the blue cheese dressing
but thicker.
*Better plan to make extra batch, it is that
good*

*A CREATIVE MAN IS MOTIVATED BY THE
DESIRE TO ACHIEVE,
NOT BY THE DESIRE TO BEAT OTHERS.*
Ann Rand

LIMA BEAN HUMMUS

2 cups lima beans
2 cloves garlic
2 Tb water
1 Tb olive oil or coconut oil
1 Tb sesame oil
Salt to taste / spice of choice to taste

Cook lima beans in water to cover, about 10 minutes until tender. Drain
Cool. Put first 4 ingredients in food processor until smooth.
Add sesame oil, process till smooth. Season to taste with salt and other
Spice.

VITALITY SHOWS NOT ONLY IN THE ABILITY TO PERSIST,
BUT IN THE ABILITY TO START OVER.

SPICE WHITE BEAN DIP

1 19 Oz can navy or other white beans
¾ cup liquid from beans
3 Tb lemon juice
2 tsp minced garlic
1 tsp dry parsley
¼ each, black pepper; cayenne
¼ cup olive or coconut oil

Process all until smooth

RICE CRUST FOR ALL QUICHE

1 ½ Cups cooked rice
(optional - cook rice in chicken stock
   and 1 Tsp miso)
½ cup cottage cheese
1 egg white; use yolk for filling
2 Tb chopped parsley leaves or 1 Tb dry
Butter for greasing pan

Heat oven to 350 degrees
Combine all ingredients and press into
Quiche Pan, bake 10-15 minutes.
Fill with the following recipes or your own.

REAL MEN EAT QUICHE

CLAMS CASINO

25 cherry or medium clams
1 onion, chopped
1 bell pepper, chopped
4-5 strips bacon, cut into 1/2 inch strips
Dash cayenne

Cool clams for easy opening. Open and chop clams. Mix clam juice, chopped clams with onions and peppers, put spoonful in clam shells. Lay two strips of bacon over each with a dash of cayenne. Broil for 5 minutes.

SEAFOOD QUICHE

Rice crust (see recipe)
9-10 ounce bag spinach, or frozen spinach
1 Tb olive oil
1-2 cloves garlic, chopped
¼ cup onion, chopped
4 eggs, plus the 1 egg yolk left from pie crust
1 pint ½ and ½ cream
12 shrimp, other fish or both, cut into pieces
½ cup flour
1 tsp Old Bay seasoning
8 ounces extra sharp cheese or cheese of choice, shredded
Salt and pepper to taste
Little dry red pepper to taste (optional)
Paprika to sprinkle over top
Sauté spinach in 1 Tb olive oil until almost no liquid left, mix in onions and garlic, sauté a little longer (do not burn).
Put 1/2 cup flour, Old Bay, salt, pepper in plastic bag or other covered container. Throw shrimp and or other sea food in bag, shake to cover all.
In large bowl put ½ and ½, cream and eggs, blend till frothy.
Layer all ingredients, start with shredded cheese on bottom, then liquid, spinach, onion, garlic mix, place seafood pieces in, shake a little dry red hot peppers, continue, finishing with a layer of cheese on top. Sprinkle paprika on top. Bake 350 for 45 minutes, or until set

SPINACH & BACON QUICHE

Rice crust for quiche

7 thick-sliced bacon
6 eggs
1 cup ½ and ½
4 Oz cream cheese
8 Oz sharp cheese (or cheese of choice)
½ cup parmesan grated
¼ cup scallions
1 clove garlic chopped
1 tsp sea salt
¼ tsp black pepper and cayenne
10 Oz chopped frozen or fresh spinach
1 Tb butter
Cook bacon until crisp, drain on paper towels.
Leave a little bacon fat in pan and sauté
spinach, scallions and garlic, mix in bacon.
Beat eggs, ½ and ½ milk, salt and cayenne to
frothy.
Shred cheese.
Layer ingredients starting with liquid, top with
cheese
Sprinkle paprika on top.
Bake 400 degrees 40 minutes or until knife
inserted in middle comes out clean.

*"IT IS OFTEN YOUR ATTITUDE AND NOT YOUR
APTITUDE THAT DETERMINES YOUR ALTITUDE"*
Jesse Jackson

TOMATO TART

Dough for 1 pie crust (or rice crust)
2 Tb olive tapenade*
2 large red tomatoes, thinly sliced
2 large green tomatoes, thinly sliced
Salt and ground black pepper to taste
1 Tb fresh thyme
1 Tb fresh rosemary

Heat oven to 375 degrees.
Spray 9 inch tart pan with olive oil cooking spray.
Roll pie crust out to 10 inch circle or use rice crust.
Press into tart pan, then lightly spray with olive oil.
Bake 10 minutes. Let cool.
Increase oven to 425 degrees.
Spread tapenade* evenly over bottom of tart shell.
Layer tomatoes, with edges overlapping.
Alternate green and red slices. Season salt, pepper thyme and rosemary.
Repeat with remaining tomatoes and seasoning.
Bake 20 minutes.
*chopped olives, thyme and olive oil

"FAILURE IS THE CONDIMENT THAT GIVES SUCCESS IT FLAVOR" Truman Capote

PEANUT BUTTER BANANA BREAD

(with chocolate chips optional)

BLEND:
3-4 bananas
1 cup sugar
1 cup chunky peanut butter
2 eggs
½ cup yogurt or butter milk
1 tsp vanilla extract

WHISK:
1 2/3 cups all-purpose flour
1 tsp ground cinnamon
(optional 1 cup chocolate chips)

Preheat oven to 350 degrees
Coat three 6x3x2 inch loaf pans with Coconut
oil.
Fold dry ingredients into wet ingredients.
DON'T OVER MIX

Bake 45-50 minutes until knife inserted into
Middle come out clean.

THE WAY TO GET STARTED IS TO
QUIT TALKING AND BEGIN DOING

Grilled Zucchini Roll-Ups

¼ cup feta cheese and or blue cheese
¼ cup cream cheese
2 Tb mayonnaise or yogurt
1 tsp fresh thyme
½ tsp oregano
1 Tb lemon juice
3 Tb olive oil, divided
Salt and black pepper to taste
10 8 inch long strips zucchini, sliced ¼ inch thick
And about 2 inches wide.

Combine all ingredients (using 1 Tb olive oil) except zucchini in a bowl.
Using remaining 2 table spoons olive oil, coat zucchini, and sprinkle with salt. Grill uncovered until tender, about 2 minutes each side. Set aside to cool. Pat dry and spread 1 tsp on each. Roll slices. Top with lemon zest and thyme.

"GOD HEALS, AND THE DOCTOR TAKES THE FEES."
Benjamin Franklin

SOUPS AND STEWS

Vegetable Soup

2 quarts V8 or tomato soup
1 carrot
1 celery
1-2 potatoes
Salt and pepper to taste

Bring to light boil, turn down temperature
simmer.
Simmer 20-30 minutes.

A cloudy day is no match for a sunny
disposition.
Or a bowl of soup.

Vegetable Of Beef Soup

2 Quarts V8 or tomato soup
½ pound chuck steak cut up
1 carrot
1 celery
1-2 potatoes
1 tsp beef bouillon
1 tsp miso
½ tsp pepper

Sauté chuck steak, mix in with rest of
ingredients bring to light boil, turn down
temperature to simmer.
Simmer 20-30 minutes.

Anything attempted remains impossible.

*So-don't be afraid to put other ingredients in
your soups.*

SWEET AND SOUR VEGETABLE SOUP

2 quarts V8 and or tomato soup
1 carrot
1 celery
1-2 potatoes
¼ wedge of cabbage cut up
½ tsp beef bouillon optional
2 Tb sugar
1-2 Tb apple cider vinegar
½ tsp pepper

Bring to light boil, turn temperature down to
simmer
Simmer half hour.

Being willing makes you able.

Go ahead, throw some other stuff in your soup.

1 beet or 1 can beets
1 clove garlic
1 can cream of chicken soup
1 tsp beef bouillon
½ tsp tarragon
½ tsp parley
1 Tb red wine vinegar
¼ tsp black white pepper
½ tsp salt
Plain yogurt

Puree beets and garlic clove in blender till smooth. Add rest of ingredients and blend. Chill, serve cold with yogurt to taste on top.

NEVER GIVE UP

Avocado Soup

2 soft avocados, pitted and peeled
1 tsp lemon juice
1 cup cold chicken broth
1 cup cream
½ cup plain yogurt (whole or low fat)
½ cup white wine
Salt to taste; dash white pepper

Put all ingredients in blender and blend until smooth.
Serve cold.

"WE JUDGE OURSELVES BY WHAT WE FEEL
CAPABLE OF DOING,

WHILE OTHERS JUDGE US BY WHAT WE HAVE
ALREADY DONE."

Henry Wadsworth Longfellow

SENATE BEAN SOUP

(old time favorite)

2 cups dry navy beans (1 pound)
12 cups water
1 ham hock, 2 pounds cut up ham
2 ½ cups diced or mashed potatoes
1 large onion chopped
1 clove garlic chopped
1 carrot chopped
2 celery stalks chopped
1 or 2 garlic cloves minced
2 tsp salt; ½ tsp white pepper (or black)

Cover beans with water and soak overnight.

Add all other ingredients, bring to boil then turn temperature down to simmer for 3 hours, or until ham falls off the bone.

Or cook in slow cooker for 5 or 6 hours.

A BLACK BELT IS A WHITE BELT THAT DIDN'T QUIT.
Grand Master E.B. Sell

1 pound dry split peas or other type of lentil
8 cups water
1 large onion chopped
2 stalks celery chopped
2 carrots chopped
1 clove garlic minced
¼ tsp white pepper (or black)
1 ham hock, 2 pounds chopped ham

Put all ingredients, except carrot, in large pot and bring to boil, reduce heat simmer for 1 ½ hours or when ham is falling off the bone.

Remove bone from ham hock, cut ham into ½ inch pieces.
Return ham and carrots to soup and simmer for another 30 minutes or so.

A CHAMPION IS A DREAMER THAT REFUSED TO GIVE UP!

LEEK AND POTATO SOUP

(a real winner)

3 large leeks, finely chopped (tops included)
¼ cup butter
1 celery stalk chopped
4 cups water
4 cups chicken stock
6 medium potatoes chopped (leave skins on optional)
2 tsp salt
⅓ tsp white pepper

Additional ¼ cup butter
½ cup heavy cream

Melt ¼ cup butter in large pot. Add leeks and celery.
Reduce heat, cover and cook for 5 minutes, or until vegetables sweat. Don't overcook. Put remaining ingredients into pot and simmer 45 minutes or until potatoes are soft. Puree in blender till smooth. To thick, put a little more chicken broth in. Add remaining ¼ cup butter and heavy cream.

UMMMMMMMM

BAKED LIMA BEANS

2 pounds dry lima beans (large or small) covered with water and soaked overnight
1 pound Italian hot sausage cut up and browned
½ pound bacon cut up and browned
1 medium onion diced
1-2 cups ketchup
3 Tb mustard
½ cup maple syrup
1 cup brown sugar
2 tsp salt
1 tsp black pepper
Dash powered cloves
Dash dry hot pepper – to taste
Dash tabasco
Dash dry habanero (optional)
4 cups water

Drain beans put in 9 5/8 x 3 ½ x 2 ¾ aluminum pan cover with 4 cups water and the rest of the ingredients. Bring to boil in 350 degree oven reduce temperature to 150-200 degrees cover and cook for 6 hours. Stir occasionally, cook to desired consistency.

To get what you want, STOP doing what isn't working.

HAM AND LIMA BEANS

3 pounds dry large lima beans (cover with
water and soak overnight)
1 ham hock and meat
1 large onion chopped
3 carrots chopped
3 celery stalks chopped
1 ½ Tb chicken stock or 5 cubes chicken
bouillon
10 potatoes chopped
½ tsp black pepper to taste
1 bay leaf; dash dry hot peppers to taste

Drain soaked beans, cover drained beans with
water. Put all other ingredients in large pot,
bring to boil and turn down to simmer for 4-6
hours, till beans are soft. Remove ham hock
and break up ham. Serve hot with a little
ketchup if desired.

EAT HEALTHY MY FRIENDS

4 cans black beans, 15 Oz each, rinsed and
drained
3 cups chicken stock
3 cups vegetable stock
1 large onion chopped
4 cloves garlic minced
1 medium sweet red pepper chopped
1 jalapeno pepper, remove seeds and mince
2 Tb olive oil
1tsp cumin
Sea salt and pepper to taste

Sauté onions and peppers in olive oil until
translucent. Add garlic and cook a little longer.
Put all ingredients in slow cooker, bring to boil,
turn down to simmer covered for 30 minutes.
Top with a little chopped onion and sour
cream.

*Excellence is doing ordinary things
extraordinarily well.*

CREAM OF ASPARAGUS SOUP

1 lbs. asparagus, cut into 2 inch pieces
1 onion chopped
4 cups chicken stock
2 Tb butter
2 Tb flour
½ cup cream
Sea salt and white pepper to taste

Sauté onion and butter to translucent. Stir in flour.
Slowly mix in chicken broth, add asparagus.
Cover and simmer 25 minutes or until asparagus is tender. Puree until smooth. Add cream, sea salt and pepper to taste.

THE BEST WAY TO PREDICT THE FUTURE IS TO INVENT IT.

6 Alarm Chili

2 big cans red kidney beans
2 big cans light kidney beans
4 cans 15 ounce pinto beans
2-3 cans crushed tomatoes
15 pounds hamburger
1 pound Italian hot sausage
1 large onion chopped
2 cloves garlic chopped
½ bell pepper chopped
1 each, long hot, banana pepper, jalapeno, all
seeded and chopped
4 Tb chili power
¼ to ½ dry habanero (be careful)
7 beef bouillon cubes
2 Tb salt

Sauté hamburger till brown (drain ¾ of fat off), sprinkle1-2 Tb corn starch over each batch as you cook (depends on frying pan size). Sauté sausage until brown.

Put all into 18 quart slow cook or large pot and simmer for 3 or 4 hours.

Great winter warmer upper.

CHILI

1 large can kidney beans and juice
2 small cans, 15 ounce, pinto beans with juice
1 cup water
3 beef bouillon cubes
1 ½ pounds hamburger
1 small link Italian hot sausage
2 Tb flour
1 can medium can chopped tomatoes
½ medium onion chopped
1 clove garlic chopped
¼ each - bell; jalapeno; sweet peppers
1 Tb chili pepper
Dash powered cloves
½ tsp black pepper
Salt to taste
Dry red peppers to taste

Sauté all meat when brown sprinkle flour over.
Put all in 4 quart slow cooker and simmer for
couple of hours.

*"You cannot open a book without learning
something."*
Confucius

CREAM OF CAULIFLOWER SOUP

1 head cauliflower broken into florets steamed
1 celery stalk chopped
2 Tb onion chopped
2 Tb honey
¾ cup water
1 tsp olive oil
¼ sea salt
White pepper to taste
1/4 tsp Tai curry paste (optional)

Puree all ingredients until smooth. Put all in
pot and slowly warm.

"When love is not madness, it is not love."
Pedro Calderon de la Barca

Miso Soup

½ cup chopped scallion
½ tsp wakame
Several pieces cubed tofu
1 cup water
2 tsp miso

Bring first 4 ingredients to boil simmer 15 minutes.
Dissolve miso in 1/3 cup hot water removed from burner, and mix miso in. Do not boil miso.

Miso Soup With Shrimp

1 package instant miso soup mix
1 romain leaf, or spinach leaf chopped
2 Tb cubed tofu
3-4 cooked shrimp

Prepare soup mix according to package
instructions.
Bring water to boil, turn down to simmer and
add romain or spinach, shrimp and tofu. About
1 or 2 minutes.

CHICKEN SOUP ON THE QUICK

1 whole (2 halves) chicken breast diced
4 cups chicken stock (regular or low sodium)
2 Tb diced shallots
1 carrot chopped
1 garlic clove minced
1 Tb olive oil
Sea salt and white pepper to taste

Heat olive oil and saute shallots and carrot, cook until shallots are translucent, add garlic, saute a little longer (do not burn garlic). Add chicken and cook, stirring, for about 1 minute. Add broth and bring to boil. Reduce heat and simmer for
2 or 3 minutes untill chicken heated through.

TOUGH TIMES NEVER LAST, BUT TOUGH PEOPLE DO.

BEEF AND BEAN STEW

2 pounds boneless beef chuck (cut into 1 inch pieces)
1 pound white mushrooms sliced
1 carrot chopped
2 celery chopped
1 medium onion chopped
2 cloves garlic minced
1 can (15 ounce) pinto beans or other white beans
1 can (28 ounce) chopped tomatoes
4 cups water
½ tsp cinnamon
1 Tb olive oil
Dash dry red pepper
Salt and black pepper to taste
Season beef with a little salt and pepper, depending on size of pan, saute all or a part at a time, utill brown. Remove to plate
Saute, mushrooms, onion, celery and carrot until translucent, add garlic. Add remaining ingredients and beef, bring to boil, turn down to simmer for about 2 hours or until beef is tender.

2 pounds sirloin steak (trim fat and cut into small pieces)
2 Tb olive oil
½ cup chopped onion
1 small sweet potato chopped
1 small parsnip chopped
1 box frozen peas
1 can chopped tomatoes (14 ounce)
2 cups beef broth
¼ tsp dried thyme or 1 Tb fresh thyme chopped
2 Tb corn starch
Sea Salt and black pepper to taste

Sauté steak in 1 Tb olive oil until brown, sprinkle corn starch over steak, remove to bowl.
Sauté onion in pot with 1 Tb olive oil until translucent, stir in steak, sweet potato, parsnip, tomatoes and beef both. Bring to boil lower temperature to simmer for 25 minutes until tender. Stir in peas, thyme, salt and pepper.

"Study the past, if you would divine the future."
Confucius

GAZPACHO

4 large tomatoes chopped
1 carrot diced small
1 stalk celery diced
1 small onion diced
1 small cucumber diced
1 medium bell pepper chopped
¼ cup lemon juice
½ cup water
½ cup olive oil
2 garlic cloves minced
2 packets stevia or 1 Tb honey
1 tsp dried basil or a leaves chopped
1 tsp sea salt
¼ tsp black or white pepper

In blender, blend tomatoes, oil, water, sea salt, pepper, garlic, basil, ¼ cup lemon juice and stevia until smooth.
Mix all together in large bowl and chill, serve chilled.

The mind attempts to limit
the Unlimited with every thought.

– Michael Jeffreys

MANHATTAN CLAM CHOWDER

2 dozen large clams chopped and juice
4 slices of bacon cut into small pieces
1 large onion diced
1 carrot diced
2 celery stalks diced
1 bell pepper diced
4 potatoes chopped, leave skin on
1 16 ounce can chopped tomatoes
1 bay leaf
1 Tb oregano
2 tsp thyme
Dash dry red peppers to taste
2 tsp black pepper
4 cups water
½ cup flour for thickening

Put clams in refrigerator to make easy opening. While clams are cooling mix all other ingredients, except flour in large pot and bring to boil, turn down and simmer for one hour. Open clams and chop, put all juice and chopped clams in pot. Bring soup to slow boil, mix flour with1/2 cup water and slowly mix into soup to thicken

SALADS AND DRESSINGS

Best Cole Slaw

1 head cabbage
¾ cup sugar (1 cup if large head or to taste)
1 cup mayonnaise
1 small onion
1 carrot
3 Tb lemon juice
3 Tb apple cider vinegar
Couple dashes Tabasco Sauce
1 Tb kosher salt or to taste
2 tsp black pepper

Chop cabbage and fill ¾ way of blender and cover with water give a couple of pulses (do not over pulse), pour into colander, continue with rest of cabbage. Put chopped onion in with one of the cabbage pulses. Chop carrot and pulse in blender. After cabbage, onion and carrot are well drained, mix in with rest of the ingredients. Cool for several hours or overnight.
QUICK WAY: buy bag of shredded cabbage with carrots, mince onion but in large bowl or pan and follow the above instructions, without the blender.

AMBROSIA

1 8 ounce package cream cheese, softened
¼ cup sugar
¼ cup milk
2 tsp vanilla extract
1 can crushed pineapple, drained
1 can mandarin oranges, drained
2 apples, chopped
1-2 cups miniature marshmallows (optional)

Mix softened cream, milk, sugar and vanilla
until well blended.
Fold in remaining ingredients. Cool for couple
of hours or overnight.

"Figure out what you are good at and how you
can make the most of the situation you are in,
and just don't look back."
Julia Chen

APPLE-CELERY SALAD

2 medium apples cored and diced
2 stalks celery, chopped
2 Tb lemon juice
1 Tb honey
½ cup chopped pecans

Combine first 4 ingredients, mix in pecans.
Cool for 1 or 2 hours and serve.
Might want to make extra.

WALDORF SALAD

2 apples cored and chopped
1 celery stalk chopped
1 carrot shredded
½ cup raisins
½ cup chopped walnuts
3-4 Tb mayonnaise or yogurt

Fold all together. That's it.
Serve cool.

STAY HEALTHY MY FRIENDS

CARROT SALAD

4 carrots shredded
1 cup raisins
½ cup mayonnaise or yogurt to taste

Mix all together, serve cool.

"WHEN ANGER RISES, THINK OF THE
CONSEQUENCES."
Confucius

NORMA'S CRANBERRY RELISH

4 bags cranberries (2-3 pounds), chopped
12 large apples, chopped
1 cup walnuts, chopped
1 cup crushed pineapple – drained
6 cups sugar
4 cups hot water
3 cups cold water
4 boxes cherry gelatin

Mix sugar, hot water and gelatin. Stir in rest of the ingredients. Refrigerate for several hours. Freeze if you like.

Easy way to chop apples and cranberries. Core and slice apples put into blender, cover with water and pulse couple of times. Do same with cranberries. BE CAREFUL DON'T OVER PULSE OR YOU WILL HAVE JUICE.

"SPEAK THE TRUTH, DO NOT YIELD TO ANGER, GIVE, IF THOU ART ASKED FOR LITTLE BY THESE THREE STEPS THOU WILT GO NEAR THE GODS."
Confucius

BROCCOLI SALAD

2 stalks broccoli, cut into pieces
1 1 small sweet onion, chopped
1 pound bacon, cooked and crumbled
1 cup mayonnaise
¾ cup sugar
½ cup apple cider vinegar

Mix broccoli, onion and carrot. Blend
mayonnaise, sugar and vinegar, fold into
broccoli mixture. Refrigerate for hour or two
and serve.

*"THE ESSENCE OF KNOWLEDGE IS, (IF) HAVING
IT, TO APPLY IT, (IF) NOT HAVING IT, CONFESS
YOUR IGNORANCE."*
Confucius

TUNA SALAD

1 can tuna (6-7 ounce)
1 stalk celery chopped
Mayonnaise to taste
¼ tsp oregano or to taste
¼ tsp black pepper or to taste
Dash sea salt
Shake dried red peppers

Mix all together, refrigerate.
Serve as salad, dip or make sandwich.

*"LEARNING WITHOUT THOUGHT IS LABOR
LOST.
THOUGHT WITHOUT LEARNING IS PERILOUS"*
Confucius

FLORIDA FRUIT SALAD

1 head lettuce or romaine
1 grapefruit
2 oranges
¼ cup sweet fruit dressing

Peal grapefruit and orange, cut into bite size
pieces.
Break lettuce or romaine into bite size pieces.
Put fruit over lettuce or romaine, drizzle
dressing over to taste.

SWEET FRUIT DRESSING

½ cup sugar
¼ cup apple cider vinegar
1 tsp salt
1 tsp dry mustard
1 tsp paprika
1 tsp minced onion
1 cup extra virgin olive oil or vegetable oil

Place all, except oil, in blender. Turn blender
on to medium and slowly poor oil in until thick.

*"A FOOL DESPISES GOOD COUNSEL, BUT A
WISE MAN TAKES IT TO HEART."*
Confucius

Eggless Egg Salad

1 package fine tofu
3 Tb mayonnaise or plain yogurt
¼ tsp honey
¼ tsp turmeric
Dash dry mustard
Dash sea salt
2 Tb sweet relish
2 Tb scallions minced
2 Tb celery chopped fine
White pepper to taste

Dry tofu on paper towels. Crumble tofu or chop into small pieces. Mix all other ingredients add tofu and continue to mix. Cool in refrigerator.

APPLE, RASPBERRY AND YOGURT SALAD

DRESSING:
2 ½ Tb extra- virgin olive oil
1/1/2 Tb rice vinegar or apple cider vinegar
1 Tb lime juice
½ tsp honey or agave nectar
1 tsp Dijon mustard
Dash sea salt and black pepper to taste
3 cups vanilla yogurt

SALAD:
1 apple chopped
¾ cup raspberries
2 Tb feta cheese crumbled
1 bag mixed greens

Make dressing in separate bowl, cool. Toss
salad ingredients in large bowl. Drizzle
dressing over.

ENJOY

GERMAN POTATO SALAD

4 medium red bliss or white potatoes
3 slices bacon cut into strips and sauté to
brown
1 medium onion, chopped (1/2 cup)
1 Tb sugar
1 Tb flour
½ tsp sea salt
Dash black pepper
¼ cup apple cider vinegar
½ cup water

Put potatoes in pot, cover with water bring to
boil, reduce heat, cover and simmer for 30—
35 minutes. Drain and let cool a little, slice or
cut into bite size.

Sauté onion in bacon fat, when translucent,
stir in sugar, flour, and pepper. Stir constantly
until thickened. Stir water and vinegar in,
bring to boil, stir for 1 minute.

Mix potatoes and bacon into mixture and heat
to bubbly.

"I NEVER SAID MOST OF THE THINGS I SAID"
Yogi Berra

CUCUMBER SALAD

2 medium cucumbers, sliced thin
1 small onion, slice thin
1/3 cup vinegar
1/3 cup water
2 Tb sugar
½ tsp sea salt
Dash or two pepper

Place cucumbers and onions in bowl. Mix all other ingredients, stir into cucumbers and onions. Cover and put In refrigerator for several hour and or overnight. Use large slotted spoon to serve.

DO WHAT YOU CAN DO WITH WHAT YOU HAVE

DIJON DRESSING

2 tsp Dijon mustard
4 tsp red wine vinegar
1 tsp honey
1 garlic clove minced
½ cup extra virgin olive oil
1 tsp water
Dash sea salt and white pepper

Place all ingredients in blender and mix on medium speed.

"GO TO HEAVEN FOR THE CLIMATE, HELL FOR COMPANY."
                    Mark Twain

FRENCH DRESSING

3 Tb vinegar
½ tsp Worcestershire sauce
1 clove garlic minced
Dash of Tabasco sauce
1 Tb horse-radish
½ cup extra virgin olive oil
½ tsp sea salt
Dash black pepper

Blend all on medium speed.

*"HEALTH IS THE GREATEST GIFT,
CONTENTMENT THE GREATEST WEALTH,
FAITHFULNESS THE BEST RELATIONSHIP."*
Buddha

APPLE PLUM CHUTNEY

1½ cups apple cider vinegar
1½ cups sugar
3½ cups granny smith apples, peeled, cored
and chopped
½ pound plums, cored and sliced into ½ pieces
1 large sweet onion chopped
1 jalapeno pepper, minced with seeds
1 carrot chopped
2 cinnamon sticks
2 cloves garlic, minced
1 Tb fresh ginger, minced
Dash cayenne
½ tsp dry mustard
1 tsp sea salt
1 bay leaf
½ cup white raisins

Boil vinegar and sugar. When sugar is
dissolved, lower heat to simmer, add all other
ingredients, except raisins and plums, simmer
for 30 minutes, add raisins and plums, cook for
another10 minutes or until chutney has
thickened. Cool for a couple of hours, remove
cinnamon stick and bay.

*"WHAT YOU DO TODAY, CAN IMPROVE YOUR
TOMORROW."*
R. Marston

Chicken Salad

1-2 cups chicken, chopped or 1 can 13 ounce
can of chicken
½ cup mayonnaise
1 celery stalk chopped
¼ sweet onion chopped (optional)
Dash parsley
Dash cayenne
½ tsp sea salt
Black pepper to taste

Mix all ingredients, refrigerate to cool.

CAJUN COLESLAW

1 bag shredded cabbage about 3 cups
1 carrot shredded
½ cup mayonnaise
½ sweet onion minced
1 Tb apple cider vinegar
2 tsp horseradish
Dash cayenne, to taste

Mix all ingredients in large bowl. Cool in refrigerator.

Follow not in the footsteps of the masters, but rather seek what they sought.

WILD RICE AND APPLE SALAD

1 cup uncooked wild rice
2 cups vegetable broth or apple juice
2 large apples, cored and chopped
1 Tb lemon juice
1 Tb brown sugar
2 stalks celery, chopped
1 cup plain yogurt or vanilla yogurt
½ cup mayonnaise

Cook rice in broth, according to recipe on rice packet. Drain rice if necessary and cool. Mix apples with lemon juice, brown sugar, and celery. Toss with wild rice, yogurt and mayonnaise.

*MARTIAL ARTIST FIND WHAT THEY SEEK,
BUT IT IS NOT WHAT THEY EXPECTED*
Me

WALNUT DRESSING

½ cup toasted walnuts, chopped
½ cup fruit, raspberry; blue berry, strawberry,
etc.
¼ cup red wine vinegar
2 Tb honey
1 Tb Dijon mustard
½ cup extra virgin olive oil
Dash of sea salt and pepper to taste

Put all ingredients, except olive oil, in blender
and blend until smooth. Drizzle oil in until
smooth.

THREE BEAN SALAD

1 can cut green beans
1 can kidney beans
1 can cut wax beans
1 cup extra virgin olive oil
3 sweet onions, chopped
2 cloves garlic, minced
2 Tb sugar

Mix all beans and onions. Mix oil, garlic and sugar. Pour over beans and onions, toss together. Refrigerate for several hours or overnight, to blend flavors.

'ALWAYS DO YOUR BEST.
WHAT YOU PLANT NOW,
YOU WILL HARVEST LATER."
Og Mindiono

Blue Cheese Dressing

4 ounce sour cream
4 ounce mayonnaise or yogurt
2 packages crumbled blue cheese
¼ onion minced
Pinch salt and white pepper

Mix all together and refrigerate for couple of hours.

"PROCRASTINATION IS THE ART OF KEEPING UP WITH YESTERDAY.
Don Marquis

MAIN COURSE
AND
SIDES

ROAST CHICKEN

(let's keep it simple)

1 roasting chicken 6-8 pounds
1 stalk celery, cut into 3 inch pieces
1 carrot, cut into 3 inch pieces
1 small onion, quartered
Extra virgin olive oil
Salt, pepper, garlic power, paprika and poultry
seasoning to taste

Cut tail off and most of the fat from the
bottom side of chicken. Rinse chicken off and
pat a little dry. Place in roasting pan. Put cut
up celery, carrot and onion in chicken cavity.
Sprinkle all dry seasonings to taste over
chicken.
With your hand, rub extra virgin olive oil over
seasonings and chicken.
Bake according to time on package chicken
came in. That's it, don't mess with it, don't
cover it, leave it alone and let it cook. You will
have a nice golden, moist chicken. ENJOY

THERE ARE NO SHORT CUTS
GOING TO A PLACE WORTH GOING

MASH POTATO WITH TURNIP

5 large russet or white potatoes, cut up
1/2 turnip cut up
Chicken bouillon to cover
4 Tb butter
¼ cup milk
1 garlic clove, minced
1 tsp olive oil
2 tsp sea salt or to taste
1 tsp pepper or to taste

Put potatoes (leave skins on - optional) and turnips in separate pots, cover and bring to boil, turn down to simmer for about 30 minutes. Turnips take a little longer. Drain (keep a little of liquid for thinning if needed). Put garlic and olive oil in very small bowl, microwave for about 15 to 30 seconds. Mash potatoes and turnips. Mash rest of ingredients in.

UNCLE JIMS BAR B Q

14-16 pounds pork butts or beef bottom roast
1 large onion, chopped
2 carrots, shredded
2 cloves garlic, minced
1-quart ketchup
1 cup mustard
½ cup brown sugar
¼ cup vinegar
3Tb chili power
¼ cup kosher salt
1 Tb black pepper
¼ tsp Tabasco or to taste
1 tsp dry red pepper or to taste

Cut a little of fat off the meat and put into an
18 quart slow cooker. Mix rest of ingredients
and pour over meat. Bring to boil, then turn
down to simmer for 4-5 hours. Remove any
bones and any large pieces of fat. Cut and
shred meat. Serve as is, on a bun, with or
without coleslaw. Serves 25-30.

DÉJÀ VU ALL OVER AGAIN
Yogi Barra

ZUCCHINI CRAB CAKES

2 cups zucchini, seeds removed and shredded
1 ½ cup seasoned panko
1 egg beaten
1 tsp Old Bay seasoning
1 Tb mayonnaise
1 small onion, minced
Dash cayenne
Dash black pepper
Vegetable oil for frying

Mix all ingredients in a bowl. Form into 4 or 5 round patties.
Fry in vegetable oil until brown on both sides, 3-4 minutes, or bake 350 degree oven for 25 minutes.

"It is man's own mind, not his enemy
or foe that lures him to evil ways."
Buddha

Potato Latkes

5 baking potatoes or russet
¼ medium onion, chopped
1 egg, beaten
1 clove garlic, minced
¼ cup Bisquick
1 tsp sea salt
Black pepper to taste
Vegetable oil, for frying

Shred potatoes, strain, pressing down with a
spoon. Pour water off, keep starch on bottom
if desired. Mix all ingredients together. With
large spoon, drop mixture into heated oil.
Brown both sides. Drain on paper towels.
Serve with apple sauce, sour cream or plain.

SCALLOPED EGGPLANT

(a meal in itself)

1 large eggplant, diced
1/3 cup milk
1 can condensed cream of mushroom soup (10 ½ ounce)
1 egg, slightly beaten
½ cup onion, chopped
¾ cup herb stuffing
Dash of dry red pepper, optional
 Cheese Topper
½ cup herb stuffing
2 Tb butter melted
4 ounces sharp cheese or cheese of your choice, shredded   Paprika

Set oven temperature to 350 degrees.
Cook diced eggplant in boiling salted water till tender, 6-7 minutes, drain. In 10x6x2 inch baking dish, mix milk, soup and egg. Add eggplant, onion and stuffing and combine. For cheese topper, grind stuffing until crumbly, add butter, mix. Sprinkle over casserole. Top with cheese, sprinkle paprika over top. Bake 350 degrees for 20-25 minutes.
Makes 6-8 servings. Or maybe one?

"WHAT WE THINK WE BECOME"
Buddha

Easy Stroganoff

1 pound ground beef
3 slices bacon, cut in strips
½ onion, minced
1 can cream of mushroom soup (10 ½ ounces)
1 cup milk
1 beef bouillon cube
2 Tb flour
1 tsp powered garlic
1 tsp paprika
1 cup sour cream
1 can evaporated milk (6 ounces)
2 Tb dry sherry

Brown ground beef and bacon in large frying pan, drain most of the fat. Put onion in and cook a little longer. In bowl combine milk, soup, garlic power, sour cream and evaporated milk. Pour into frying pan, mixing with meat and onion. Bring to light boil. Mix flour with 1/4 cup milk, slowly blend into frying pan until thickened. Serve over prepared noodles.

"YOU CAN OBSERVE A LOT BY WATCHING"
Yogi Barra

ZUCCHINI MEATBALLS

3 cups zucchini, grated and patted dry
1½ cup seasoned panko
1/3 cup Parmesan cheese
1 egg slightly beaten
1 garlic clove, minced
Dash cayenne, optional
Salt and pepper to taste
Olive oil for frying

Mix all ingredients, except frying oil, together.
Form into balls or patties. If too wet, add
more panko or seasoned bread crumbs.
Brown in oil on all sides. Serve with marinara,
or tomato gravy. Spoon over spaghetti, or?
 Another idea, make brown beef gravy and
serve over meatballs with mashed potatoes,
etc.
OK OK, here is another, make chicken gravy, or
cream of chicken soup and serve over
something with meatballs.

TURKEY- SPINACH CASSEROLE

1 pound ground turkey
1 onion chopped
1 can cream celery soup; mushroom or
asparagus (10.5 ounce)
1 box frozen spinach
1 clove garlic minced
2 eggs, beaten
1 pound mozzarella cheese shredded, or
cheese of choice
1 tsp sea salt
½ tsp pepper or to taste
Paprika

Heat oven to 350 degrees.
Brown turkey and onion, drain. Stir in soup
and simmer. Cook spinach according to box
instructions, drain. Add eggs, salt, pepper and
garlic, mix well. Lightly coat 9x13x2 inch
baking dish with coconut oil. Spread meat
mixture on bottom of dish. Pour spinach
mixture over meat. Top with cheese of choice.
Sprinkle paprika over cheese. Bake25-30
minutes or until cheese is melted. HINT, PUT
CHEESE IN FREEZER FOR A FEW MINUTES,
BEFORE SHREDDING.

"IN ORDER TO SUCCEED,
WE MUST FIRST BELIEVE THAT WE CAN"
K. Kazantzakis

CHICKEN POMODORO

2 boneless chicken breasts, skinned, cut into cutlets,
Put cutlets in plastic bag and pound until thin.
2 Tb olive oil
½ cup vodka
1½ cup chicken broth
¼ cup lemon juice
½ cup tomatoes, chopped
¼ cup heavy cream
½ cup sliced scallions
¼ cup water   2 Tb corn starch
Sea salt and pepper to taste
Plain Panko for covering chicken cutlets

Mix tomatoes; scallions; lemon juice into broth, set aside. Salt and pepper chicken cutlets on one side, coat with Panko, sauté in olive oil. Remove to plate. Deglaze frying pan with vodka, (away from heat); return to heat, cook until nearly evaporated. Add broth, bring to boil, mix water and cornstarch, and slowly mix into broth to thicken, stir in heavy cream. When thickened return cutlets. Serve with spaghetti or by themselves.

"PROBLEMS ARE NOT STOP SIGNS, THEY ARE GUIDE LINES"
R.H. Schuller

CHICKEN PICANTE

2 boneless chicken breasts, skinned, cut into cutlets,
Put cutlets in plastic bag and pound until thin.
Flour or panko to coat cutlets
2 Tb olive oil
¼ cup white wine
2 garlic cloves, minced
1½ cups chicken broth
¼ cup water 2 Tb cornstarch
1/3 cup lemon juice
2 Tb capers, drained
6 Tb butter
Flour or panko
Salt and pepper to taste
Sliced lemons, if desired

Microwave chicken broth for 3 minutes, mix in, lemon juice and capers. Season cutlets with salt and pepper on one side, dredge in flour or panko. Put oil in frying pan and sauté cutlets until brown on both sides, remove to plate. Deglaze frying pan with wine, add garlic, sauté a little longer (do not burn garlic). Add broth, bring to light boil. Mix cornstarch with ¼ cup cold water, slow blend into broth until thickened. Place lemon slices in broth, if desired. Blend in butter. Put cutlets into broth, coating both sides. Serve with pasta or choice of vegetables.

4 pounds chuck, cut into 1 inch cubes
½ cup flour
½ tsp dry mustard
¼ tsp paprika
1 tsp salt
½ tsp pepper
6 Tb shortening
4 beef bouillon cubes
5 cups water
1½ cups chopped onions
2 10 ounces frozen peas and carrots
2 tsp dry parsley
2 tubes buttermilk biscuits, 8 ounce each

Brown meat in shortening. Put flour, mustard, paprika, salt, and pepper in plastic bag. Toss in browned meat to cover. Dissolve bouillon in water. Combine all with onions. Cover and bake at 375 degrees for one hour and a quarter, stir in peas and carrots, bake uncovered another 15 minutes. Increase temperature to 450 degrees. Put biscuits on top, bake till brown on top, 10 to 15 minutes.

"WITH THE NEW DAY COMES NEW STRENGTHS AND NEW THOUGHTS."
Eleanor Roosevelt

LAYERED MEATLOAF

1 ½ pounds ground beef
1 egg, slightly beaten
½ cup dry bread crumbs or 1 cup panko
½ cup milk
1½ tsp salt
½ tsp pepper
DRESSING
2 cups soft bread, cut into cubes
1 stalk celery, chopped
1 Tb dry onion or ¼ cup onion chopped
1 tsp dry parsley
1 Tb water
1 tsp salt
Black pepper to taste
1 egg, slightly beaten

Heat oven to 350 degrees. Combine meatloaf ingredients. Mix dressing in bowl. Press half of meat mixture in 9x5 inch loaf pan. Top with dressing. Put rest of meatloaf on top, press down a little to form loaf. Bake 350 degrees for one hour. Cool 5 minutes, loose edges and turn out of pan. Put favorite topping on, ketchup, barbecue or type of sauce.

"I CAN RESIST EVERYTHING, EXCEPT TEMPTATION."
Oscar Wilde

SAUSAGE AND PEPPERS

1 lb. Italian sausage, mild, hot or both cut into
1 inch pieces
1 large onion, sliced
1 clove garlic, minced
2 bell peppers; 2 red peppers, sliced into strips
2 tsp dry rosemary
½ tsp oregano
Salt and pepper to taste
2 Tb olive oil

Sauté sausage in olive oil. Mix rest of
ingredients in, except salt and pepper. Turn
heat down slightly, stir occasionally until
peppers are a little limp. Add salt and pepper
if desired, remember sausage has salt and
pepper in it. Serve warm.

VEAL OR CHICKEN PARMESAN

3-4 ounces Veal cutlets or 2 chicken skinless
breast quartered
Pound meat until thin*.
2 eggs slightly beaten
Seasoned panko
Provolone, parmesan or mozzarella for melting
on top of cutlets
2 Tb olive oil
Spaghetti or Marinara sauce

Dip cutlets in eggs, use teaspoon to sprinkle
panko over both sides of cutlets. Sauté both
sides in olive oil until brown on both sides,
place cheese slices of choice over each cutlet,
continue to cook until cheese melts a little.
Serve with sauce over cutlet and spaghetti.
*PUT CUTLETS IN PLASTIC BAG AND POUND.

"I 'AM SORRY, IF YOU WERE RIGHT, I AGREE
WITH YOU."

POT ROAST BEEF

3-4 pound bottom roast beef
4 russet or baking potatoes, quartered, leave skins on
1 cup water
3 carrots, cut into 2 inch pieces
1 celery stalk, cut into 1 inch pieces
1 larger onion. Chopped or quartered
2 tsp beef bouillon paste or 2 beef bouillon cubes
Canadian steak seasoning
¼ cup flour

Brown all sides of beef. Coat beef with Canadian Steak Seasoning put in slow cooker with 1 cup water, cover and simmer for 3 hours. Put potatoes, carrots, celery and onion on top of beef, cover, simmer another hour or so. Drain off at least 2 cups of gravy, put in pot and bring to light boil. Mix flour in 1/2 cup cold water and stir in gravy slowly and continue to stir until thickened.

"SO I'M UGLY. SO WHAT?
NEVER SAW ANYONE HIT WITH HIS NOSE."
Yogi Barra

Brussel Sauté

12 Brussel sprouts, cut in half
2 Tb bacon fat or olive oil
Salt, pepper and garlic to taste

Sauté Brussel sprouts in fat untill browned on
both sides. Be careful, don't burn.

COD OR CRAB CAKES

2 pieces cod, about 3 inch or 1½ cups crab
1 egg, slightly beaten
2 Tb mayonnaise
1 tsp yellow mustard
2 tsp Old Bay Seasoning
1 tsp parsley
1 cup seasoned panko
Dash cayenne, optional
1 small onion, minced
Dash salt and pepper to taste
2 Tb olive oil

Mix mayonnaise, egg and mustard together.
Stir in remaining ingredients, except oil. Form
into 6 patties. Fry on both side about 5
minutes each, or until golden brown.

COCKTAIL SAUCE: 1/2 cup ketchup, 3 drops
lemon juice, 2 tsp horseradish, dash Tabasco
sauce and Old Bay Seasoning, blend together.

*"DO NOT DWELL IN THE PAST, DO NOT DREAM
OF THE FUTURE,
CONCENTRATE THE MIND ON THE PRESENT
MOMENT."*
Buddha

STUFFED PEPPERS

6 large bell peppers
1 pound hamburger
1 cup cooked rice with 1 tsp chicken paste and
1 tsp miso
1 clove garlic minced, 2 Tb onion, chopped
1 tsp sea salt
1 can (15 ounce) tomato sauce
4 ounces of cheese of choice; sharp,

Cut off small piece off stem side of pepper, remove seeds and membrane. Boil peppers in large pot for about 5 minutes.
Before cooking rice put chicken paste and 1 tsp miso in boiling water to dissolve, add rice and cook according to instructions.
Sauté hamburger until brown, add onion, cook until translucent; drain fat off. Stir in rice, salt, garlic and 1 cup tomato sauce. Keep hot. Stuff peppers with rice and beef mixture. Place peppers, stuffing side up, in 8x8x8x2 baking dish. Spoon remaining tomato sauce over peppers.
Cover and bake 350 degrees for 45 minutes, uncover and bake another 10 minutes, sprinkle cheese over top.

"NO ONE SAVES US BUT OURSELVES. NO ONE
CAN AND NO ONE MAY.
WE OURSELVES MUST WALK THE PATH."
Buddha

3 pounds hamburger
2 Tb cornstarch
1 carrot chopped
1 celery chopped
1 small onion chopped
1 clove garlic minced
2 tsp beef bouillon paste
2 cups hot water
½ tsp salt
¼ tsp pepper
Mashed potatoes for topping:
Use dried potatoes to make 3 cups.
Paprika

Sauté hamburger until brown, sprinkle cornstarch over and stir, put onions in, continue to sauté until onions are translucent, add garlic sauté a little longer. Mix beef bouillon paste with hot water, mix all ingredients together in a 3-4 quart baking dish. Bake 400 degrees until thickened, about 10 minutes. Spread mashed potatoes on top, sprinkle paprika over top. Lower temperature to 350 degrees and continue to bake for about 20 minutes.

"IT GETS LATE EARLY OUT HERE."
Yogi Berra

SWEET AND SOUR STIR FRY

2 half breast chicken, skinned, cut into bite sizes
Bragg's Amino or soy sauce, for marinate
¾ cup cranberries or 2 Tb apple cider vinegar
1 can (15 ounce) chunk pineapple and juice
1 clove garlic minced
1 Tb ginger shredded
1 carrot cut to bite size
1 celery cut to bite size
1 tsp Thai curry paste
1 Tb honey or sugar or brown sugar
3 Tb olive oil
2 Tb cornstarch , ¼ cup cold water

Mix cut chicken with amino or soy sauce, let marinate while preparing vegetables. Put olive oil in wok or other type frying pan. Sauté Thai curry past, garlic and ginger until blended. Throw all the vegetables in and sauté for a few minutes, continuing to stir (don't overcook), remove to a large bowl.
Put all chicken and liquids in wok and sauté until tender, pour vegetables over chicken and continue to cook for a few minutes. Mix cornstarch with ¼ cup cold water, slowly pour over all and stir until a little thickened.
TIRED? THAT'S GOOD.
NOW WE CAN TRAIN A LITTLE HARDER
Me

JAMBALAYA

1 large onion chopped
1 medium green pepper, chopped
2 celery stalks, chopped
1 can (25 ounce) diced tomatoes, don't drain
2 cloves garlic, chopped
1 tsp dried thyme
2 Tb chopped parsley, or 1 tsp dry
8 ounces cooked smoked sausage (andouille)
1 tsp each: salt; pepper and hot pepper sauce
12 peeled-deveined raw medium shrimp

Mix all ingredients, except shrimp and parsley, in 4 quart slow cooker, covered, cook for 6 hours or until vegetables are tender. Stir In shrimp and cook another 20 minutes. Serve over rice.

"You will not be punished for your anger, you will be punished by your anger."
Buddha
Or for not having enough Jambalaya

CHEESEBURGER PIE

1 pound ground beef
1 large onion, chopped
1 clove garlic, minced
1 tsp sea salt
1 cup shredded cheese
Topping
½ cup Bisquick Mix
1 cup milk
2 egg
½ cup mushroom soup

Grease 9 inch pie plate
Brown beef add onion and cook until onions are translucent, add garlic, salt and stir. Spoon into pie plate, sprinkle cheese over meat. In a bowl mix milk, eggs and soup, fold in Bisquick. Pour over meat mixture. Sprinkle paprika over top. Bake 350 degrees for 25-30 minutes.

If you want to slow time, watch the clock.

DESSERTS AND OTHER SWEETS

BROWN RICE PUDDING

2 cups cooked brown rice
3 cups almond or walnut milk*
2 Tb Splenda or stevia equivalent
3 large eggs
1 Tb vanilla extract
¼ cup maple syrup
2 tsp cinnamon
½ cup raisins soaked in 1 Tb rum

Combine all ingredients except maple syrup in
sauce pan. Cook stirring constantly until boil,
turn down, stir occasionally until thick, and
add syrup. Serve warm or cold.
*See recipes for milk.

THE BEST THINGS IN LIFE AREN'T THINGS

Last Minute Desert

1 commercial pound or butter cake
Red or white wine or syrup of choice
Cool Whip

Cut cake into 10-12 - ½ inch pieces.
Sprinkle 1 Table spoon of wine over each, put
dollop of Cool Whip over each and serve.

Is that quick or what?

DON'T OVER THINK THINGS

CHOCOLATE MERINGUE

3-4 large egg whites
½ cup Splenda or stevia equivalent
¼ tsp cream of tartar
2 Tb unsweetened cocoa power
3 ounces sugar-free dark chocolate finely chopped

Heat oven to 450 degrees F.
Line baking sheet with parchment paper.
Cool bowl in freezer for a few minutes, put egg whites in bowl use electric mixer and beat until frothy add sugar substitute, cream of tartar, cocoa, beet till soft peaks form. Fold in chocolate.

Drop by tablespoon on parchment, leave space between drops. Put in oven and turn oven off, leave for 2-3 hours.
Enjoy

THINGS IN LIFE CAN BE SIMPLE

TIRAMISU

1 package (8 ounces) cream cheese, softened
½ cup powdered sugar
2 Tb light rum or ½ tsp rum extract
1 cup heavy cream, or whipping cream
1 package ladyfingers
½ cup cold espresso or strong coffee
1 Tb Kahlua (optional) coffee liquor
2 tsp baking cocoa

Using electric mixer, beat cream cheese and
powdered sugar in large bowl until smooth,
beat in rum.
Put smaller bowl in freezer for a few minutes
remove and using an electric mixer beat cream
until stiff peaks form. Fold into cream mixture.

Separate ladyfingers, put half, cut side up, in
8x8 or 9x9 pan or baking dish. Drizzle ¼ cup
coffee (with or without Kalua) over ladyfingers.
Spread half cream cheese mixture over
ladyfingers. Put remaining ladyfingers on top,
repeat above.
Sift cocoa over top. Cover and cool a few hours
in refrigerator.

*"THERE IS MUCH PLEASURE TO BE GAINED
FROM USELESS KNOWLEDGE."*
Bertrand Russell

Orange Tiramisu

1 package cream cheese (8 ounces), softened
½ cup powdered sugar
2 Tb orange liquor (Grand Marnier) or ½ tsp orange extract
1 cup heavy cream or whipping cream
1 commercial pound or butter cake
¾ cup orange juice
2 tsp baking coco

Using electric mixer beat cream cheese and powdered sugar in large bowl until smooth, beat in orange liquor.
Put smaller bowl in freezer and cool couple of minutes, remove and using an electric mixer beat cream until stiff peaks form. Fold cream into cream cheese mixture.
Cut cake into 12 equal pieces (about ½ inch each), put 6 pieces in 8x8 or 9x9 inch pan or baking dish. Spoon half of orange juice over each, spread half of cream cheese mixture over, repeat with cake and cream cheese mixture. Sift cocoa over top. Cool in refrigerator for a few hours.

PINEAPPLE UPSIDE DOWN CARROT CAKE

1 box carrot cake mix
1 can sliced pineapples
½ cup brown sugar
2 Tb butter softened
Bottle of cocktail cherries (optional)

Follow directions on box for carrot cake.
Before putting mix into baking pan or dish,
place sliced pineapples on bottom, mix butter
and brown sugar together sprinkle over
pineapples, then follow baking directions on
box. THAT'S IT

KEY LIME PIE

1 9-inch graham cracker crumb pie crust
1 can sweetened condensed milk 15 ounce
½ cup lime juice
3 egg yolks (no whites)
1 8-ounce package cream cheese, softened
3 drops green food dye (optional)

Heat oven to 350 degrees.
Combine all ingredients except pie crust and
blend until smooth. Pour mixture into pie crust
and bake 20 minutes. Cool 15 minutes and put
in refrigerator to chill.

Can't Get Easier

CHOCOLATE OREO PIE

1 9-inch Oreo premade crust
1 can sweetened condensed milk 15 ounce
2 Tb coco
3 egg yolks (no whites)
1 8-ounce package cream cheese, softened

Heat oven to 350 degrees
Combine all ingredients except pie crust and
blend until smooth. Pour mixture into pie crust
and bake 20-25 minutes.

Try same recipe with different flavors and pie
crusts. Amoretto; Butter Scotch schnapps;
Mint schnapps, etc.

*Yep – same as key lime pie with different
flavors.*

PINEAPPLE MERINGUE PIE

1 cup sugar
2 Tb cornstarch
1/8 tsp salt
1 can crushed pineapple (20 ounce) undrained
1 Tb lemon juice
3 eggs separated
¼ tsp cream of tartar, 6 Tb sugar
1 9-pie shell, baked

I large sauce pan combine 1 cup sugar, cornstarch and salt. Stir in pineapple until blended. Bring to boil, cook and stir for 2 minutes or until thickened. Remove from heat and stir 1 cup of hot filling into egg yolks; return to pan, bring to boil, stirring constantly to thicken, about 2 minutes. Remove from heat and stir in lemon juice. Keep warm.
Meringue: cool bowl in freezer for couple of minutes. Put egg whites and cream of tartar in bowl (important - absolutely no yolk in whites, or you have to start over with fresh egg whites) beat with electric mixer until soft peaks form. Gradually beat in sugar on high until stiff peaks form.
Pour hot mixture into pie shell. Spread meringue over hot filling, make sure to seal edges to the crust. Bake 350 degrees for 15 minutes until meringue is golden brown. Cook 1 hour on rack; refrigerate for several hours before cutting.

Shoe-Fly Pie

1 unbaked pie shell (or not)

<u>For the crumb part:</u>
14 cup shortening
1 ½ cups flour
1 cup brown sugar
Work together into crumbs

<u>Liquid part:</u>
¾ tsp baking soda
1/8 tsp nutmeg
Dash each of ginger, cinnamon and cloves
¼ tsp salt
¾ cup molasses
¾ cup hot water
Mix dry ingredients well add hot water.

Combine the crumbs and liquid in alternate layers, with crumbs on bottom and top. Bake 15 minutes at 450 degrees, then 20 minutes at 350.

DESERT SALAD

1 ambrosia apple, chopped
1 carrot, shredded
½ cup raisins
¼ cup walnuts or pecans, chopped
½ cup yogurt, or vanilla yogurt
3 packets stevia

Mix all ingredients, refrigerate for a few hours or overnight, can be served right away. With a little less stevia serve as salad.

when life KNOCKS
You DOWN,
You can CHOOSE
whether or not
to get BACK uP

STEVIA RICE PUDDING

1 packet stevia
5 drops liquid stevia
2 eggs, lightly beaten
2 cups cooked jasmine rice
2 cups milk or almond milk
1/3 cup raisins
2 tsp vanilla extract
¼ tsp cinnamon
¼ tsp sea salt

Mix all ingredients, except rice, in 2 quart casserole dish. Stir in rice. Bake 350 degrees for 1 hour or until firm. Refrigerate for a few hours to cool.

Better than a thousand hollow words,
is one word that brings peace.
Buddha

Banana Cake

3 cups pastry flour
1 tsp stevia power
1 packet stevia
4 tsp baking power
1 cup almond milk
3 eggs, separated
3 tsp vanilla extract
6 Tb vegetable oil
¼ tsp sea salt
2 over ripe bananas mashed
½ cup nuts (walnut or pecans) chopped for frosting

Sift all dry ingredients. Beat egg whites until stiff, in a bowl that was cooled in freezer for a few minutes. Stir rest of ingredients together, add dry ingredients and beat to combine. Fold in beaten egg whites. Oil and flour 2 – 8 inch cake pans. Pour ingredients, equally into cake pans. Preheat oven to 350 degrees and bake for 30 minutes, or until toothpick inserted in middle, comes out dry. Cool for 10 minutes, remove to racks to finish cooling. Frosting as desired, (see frosting recipes)

"To be idle is a short road to death and to be diligent is a way of life;
foolish people are idle, wise people are diligent."
Buddha

BUTTERCREAM FROSTING

1 packet stevia power
6 drops liquid stevia
4 ounces cream cheese, softened
2 tsp vanilla extract
2 Tb dry milk
1 cup water
3 Tb cornstarch
¼ cup butter, softened
2 tsp vanilla extract
Few drops lemon extract

Mix stevia, cornstarch, dry milk and water,
heat in pan until thickened, stirring constantly.
Cool down while beating rest of ingredients for
a few minutes. Beat in cooled cornstarch
mixture. Cool further if necessary.

Be innovative and try different spices and
flavors in above recipe.

"It ain't over till it's over."
Yogi Barra

BLUEBERRY OR PEACH COBBLER

4 pints blueberries or 8 peaches, pealed
1 cup sugar
2 Tb cornstarch
1 recipe Bisquick shortcake or roll of cinnamon
buns
Dash sugar and cinnamon to sprinkle on top

Mix blueberries or peaches with sugar in an
8x12x2 casserole dish, sprinkle cornstarch over
and continue to stir. If using peaches, sprinkle
cinnamon over them. Bake in 425 degree oven
bring to boil mixing occasionally until
thickened. Remove from oven, using side of
fork spread dollops of shortcake mixture over
top, sprinkle with sugar and cinnamon. If using
cinnamon buns, unwrap and put strips over
mixture. Bake 400 degrees until top is golden
brown, about 20 minutes.

*"There are in nature neither rewards nor
punishments;
there are consequences."*
Robert Ingersoll

MERINGUE KISSES

4 egg whites, at room temperature
¼ tsp salt
¼ tsp cream of tartar
1 cup sugar
¾ tsp vanilla or 1/4 almond extract
1 or 2 drops food coloring (optional)
Your choice of color (kids probably want
purple or black)

Cool bowl in freezer for a few minutes.
Preheat oven to 250 degrees. Line baking
sheet with foil. Beat eggs in cooled bowl until
foamy mix in cream of tartar and salt. Slowly
beat in sugar, 1 Tb at a time until stiff picks are
formed. Add flavoring and coloring. Drop by
rounded teaspoonful about 2 inches apart on
baking sheet. Bake 35-40 minutes until firm.
Cool, enjoy.

*"Under democracy, one party always devotes
its chief energies to trying to prove that the
other party is unfit to rule-and both commonly
succeed, and are right."*
J.L. Mencken

Mocha Crème Brulee

3 single packs hot cocoa mix
1 cab evaporated milk, divided
2/3 cup liquid egg substitute
½ cup sugar
½ tsp expresso coffee

In blender, combine cocoa mix and ½ milk.
Pulse, scraping sides until blended. Add
remaining milk and egg substitute. Blend until
smooth. Lightly oil 6 ramekins or other small
baking dishes. Divide in equal amounts cocoa
mix into ramekins. Put in pan and fill half way
up ramekins with water. Bake 350 degrees for
35 minutes or until custard is set.

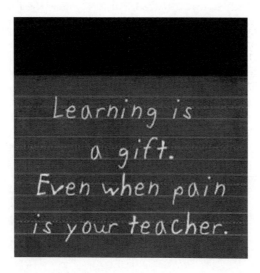

DESERT CREPES

(or use for breakfast)

1 cup milk
1 egg
1 cup Bisquick
1 packet stevia
Drop or two vanilla flavoring
Drop almond flavoring (optional)

Mix milk, egg, stevia and flavorings, blend in
Bisquick. Oil or butter a frying pan on medium.
Poor about ¼ cup mix in pan and fry about a
minute on each side. Just double ingredients if
more are desired.
Fillings to roll crepes over: Flavored yogurt,
berries, maple syrup, sour cream, etc. If
desired mix a packet of stevia in each.

YUM

LEMON BUTTER

3 eggs
1 cup sugar
5 tablespoons melted butter
Juice and grated rind of 2 lemons

Beat eggs until frothy, slowly add sugar,
continuing to beat, add butter, lemon juice
and rind. Cook in double boiler until thickened,
stirring constantly. Cool and store in
refrigerator. Use over butter cake, pound cake,
waffles, toast, etc.

PUNGENT PUMPKIN PIE

1 prepared 9 inch pie crust
16 ounce can pumpkin pie mix
12 ounce can evaporated milk
2 large eggs
¾ cup brown sugar
2 tsp hot pepper sauce or ¼ tsp cayenne
Whipped cream
¼ cup chopped pecans or walnuts

Place pie crust in pie plate. Heat oven to 400
degrees. In large bowl, combine pumpkin,
evaporated milk, eggs, brown sugar and hot
pepper sauce. With electric mixer on medium
speed, beat ingredients until well mixed. Pour
mix into prepared crust. Bake 40 to 45 minutes
until knife inserted in pie comes out clean.
Cool on wire rack. Serve with whipped cream
and chopped nuts sprinkled on top.

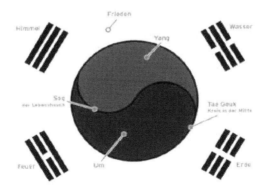

RUM BALL

2 cups vanilla wafers, fine crumb
1 cup pecans, fine chopped
1 cup confectioners' sugar
2 Tb cocoa
2 Tb corn syrup
½ cup rum or flavored brandy
Confection sugar for coating

In food processor blend all ingredients, except sugar for coating, into 1 inch balls. Coat with confection sugar. Store in air tight container for several days. Enjoy

Be careful, don't become what you don't like.
Me

GRAND MARNIER CHOCOLATE BALLS

2 cups chocolate wafers, fine crumb
1 cup almonds
1½ cups confectioners' sugar
½ cup Grand Mariner
2 Tb corn syrup
Confection sugar or cocoa for coating

Process wafers and almonds in food processor until fine. Add confectioners' sugar and process. Blend in Grand Marnier and corn syrup. Form into 1 inch balls, roll in confection sugar or cocoa to coat. Store loosely with wax paper between layers, in tight container. Let flavors blend for several days. Enjoy

"Courage is not simply one of the virtues, but the form of every virtue at the testing point."
C.S. Lewis

BEAN PIE

2 cups cooked, mashed navy beans
2 cups sugar
2 cups brown sugar
1 cup butter softened
6 eggs
2 cans evaporated milk
2 Tb vanilla
1 tsp nutmeg
1 Tb cinnamon
Dash powered clove
2 prepared pie shells

Prepare pie shells in 2 pie pan. Heat oven to 350 degrees.
Beat sugars with butter until fluffy, add eggs and milk until blended, mix rest of ingredients in. Equally divide into prepared pie shells. Bake for 45 minutes or until knife inserted in middle comes out clean.

TOMATO SOUP CAKE

2 cups flour
1 tsp baking soda
2 Tb baking powder
1¼ cup sugar
1 tsp cinnamon
½ tsp powered cloves
½ tsp nutmeg
½ tsp allspice
1 can cup condensed tomato soup
⅓ cup shortening
2 eggs
¼ cup water
1 cup walnuts, chopped
1 cup raisins

Heat oven to 350 degrees. Grease and flour 2 cake pans (8-9inch). Mix all dry ingredients together. Cream shortening and sugar, beat in soup, add eggs and water blend well. Slowly beat in dry ingredients. Stir in nuts and raisins. Divide equally between the 2 cake pans, bake for 50-60 minutes until toothpick inserted in middle comes out clean. Cool for 15 minutes and remove from pans and cool for several hours. Frost with icing of choice. Cream cheese frosting: 4 ounces cream cheese; 1 ½ cups confectioners' sugar; 1 tsp vanilla extract. Cream all together until fluffy. Frost cake.

IMPOSSIBLE CHERRY PIE

1 cup milk
2 Tb butter, softened
2 eggs
¼ tsp almond extract
¼ cup sugar
1 can (21 ounces) cherry pie filling
½ cup Bisquick mix
Streusel:
2 Tb cold butter
½ cup Bisquick mix
½ cup brown sugar
½ tsp ground cinnamon

Heat oven to 400 degrees.
Grease 10 inch pie plate. Put all ingredients in blender, except streusel and cherry pie filling, blend on high speed for 15 seconds, and pour into pie plate, spoon pie filling evenly over top. Bake for 25 minutes. While baking prepare Streusel: cut butter into Bisquick, brown sugar and cinnamon until crumbly. When pie is baked, sprinkle streusel over top and bake for another 10 minutes or until streusel is golden brown.

Try with blueberry, apple or peach pie filling with spices of choice.

PUMPKIN MINCE MEAT PIE

Makes 2 pies
2 pie crusts
1 can pumpkin pie seasoned mix
1 bottle mincemeat

Unroll pie crust and line 2-9 inch pie plates
Divide mincemeat into each pie plate, divide
pumpkin mix and spoon over mincemeat.
Bake according to pumpkin pie directions on
can

DOUBLE THE HAPPINESS

BEST BREAD PUDDING

¾ loaf of Italian or French bread cut into 1-inch cubes
3 egg yolks
3 whole eggs
1 ¾ cups sugar
4 ½ Tb vanilla extract (believe it, you will be happy)
1 tsp cinnamon
1 tsp nutmeg
½ cup softened butter
4 cups whole milk
½ cup raisins, soaked in rum or flavored brandy

Place bread cubes in ungreased 13x9x2 inch pan, toast at 350 degrees, and stir occasionally for 15 to 20 minutes until dry and golden.
In large beat, with electric mixer, whole eggs and egg yolks until frothy. Add sugar, vanilla, cinnamon and nutmeg mix well. Add softened butter and mix. Add milk and continue to mix.
Sprinkle soaked raisins over bread crumbs.
Pour milk mixture over bread. Let liquid soak into bread, push down bread to help soaking.
Bake 350 for 45 minutes.

RAVE REVIEWS

BLUE BERRY COBBLER

4 pints blue berries
1 cup sugar
2 Tb corn starch
1 recipe Bisquick shortcake recipe*
1 Tb sugar to sprinkle over top

Mix blue berries, sugar and corn starch in
13x9x2 pan.
Bake 425 to boil, remove from oven and mix.

Use side of fork to place dollops of shortcake
batter over blue berries, covering all. Sprinkle
a little sugar over top. Return to oven and
bake 15-20 minutes until top is brown.

*quick method, buy a roll of favorite cinnamon
buns, unroll buns and place over cooked blue
berry mix and follow above baking
instructions.

EXELLENCE IS NOT A SKILL. IT IS AN ATTITUDE

PEACH COBBLER

7-8 peaches (more is better)
1 cup sugar
2 Tb corn starch
3 tsp cinnamon
Dash allspice; cloves
1 recipe Bisquick shortcake recipe *
1 Tb sugar to sprinkle over top
More cinnamon to sprinkle over top

Remove skins from peaches, cut up and put into 13x9x2 pan. Mix with corn starch and cinnamon. Bake 425 to boil, remove from oven and mix.

Use side of fork to place dollops of shortcake batter over peaches, cover all. Sprinkle 1 Tb sugar over top and a little cinnamon. Return to oven and bake 15-20 minutes until top is brown.

* quick method, buy a roll of favorite cinnamon buns, unroll buns and place over cooked peach mixture and follow above baking instructions.

BAKED APPLE

1 apple of choice
1 Tb chopped nuts, walnut or pecans
2 Tb maple syrup
½ tsp cinnamon
Dash cloves

Core apple, remove skin from top of apple. Stuff nuts and raisins in cored apple, pore maple syrup over nuts sprinkle cinnamon and cloves over nuts and apple.

Place in ramekin or small bowl and microwave for 2-3 minutes or to your liking.

That's it.

LAUGHTER IS THE CLOSEST DISTANCE
BETWEEN TWO PEOPLE

NUT MILKS, JUICES AND SMOOTHIES

WALNUT MILK

1/3 cup walnuts
2 Tb maple syrup
½ tsp vanilla extract
¾ cup water

In food processor or emulsifier grind nuts until very fine. Process rest of ingredients until liquefied. Need more, just keep adding same ingredients for quantity desired. Great on cereal, etc.

Cooking Tips

Brown sugar creates the flavor of butterscotch when mixed with butter. Brown sugar is not partially refined granulated sugar, but granulated sugar with a little molasses mixed back in.

ALMOND MILK

1/3 cup almonds
1 dried date, pitted
2 Tb maple syrup, or 1 packet stevia
½ tsp vanilla extract
¾ cups water

In food processor or emulsifier grind almonds until very fine add rest of ingredients, continue to process until all is liquefied. Need more, just keep adding same ingredients for quantity desired.

Cooking Tip

For vanilla extract: place a couple of vanilla beans in a jar with 1 cup of brandy or vodka, and let mixture sit for a 2 to 3 months. When you've used all the extract, use the same beans, and add more liquor to make another batch.

CASHEW MILK

1/3 cup unsalted cashews
2 Tb maple syrup
½ tsp vanilla extract
¾ cup water

In food processor or emulsifier grind cashews
until very fine. Add rest of ingredients,
continue to process until all is liquefied. Need
more, just keep adding same ingredients for
quantity desired.

ALL NUT MILKS

Mix and match. Use honey, stevia or agave for sweetener. Blend in some other dried fruit. Pinch of salt, don't think it is necessary, but, hay.

Have Fun

SUNFLOWER SEED MILK

1 cup raw sunflower seeds
2 ¼ cup water
1 Tb honey or other sweetener
1 Tb vanilla extract
10 dried dates, pitted

In blender, put sunflower seeds, 1 cup water, honey and vanilla flavoring, blend until smooth. Add dates, blend for a minute or so. Slowly blend in water until smooth.

Health Note

Sunflower seeds are an excellent source of zinc, supportive of wound healing and prostate health.

CAROB MILK

1 ½ cups almond, walnut, cashew or sunflower milk
3 Tb unsweetened carob powder
2 Tb maple syrup or sweetener of choice
Dash cayenne (optional) for hot chocolate

Blend all ingredients until smooth. Warm for hot chocolate substitute. Want to shake things up. Blend in a banana or two or three.

Think Out Of The Box

CAROB MALTED

¼ cup flaxseeds
2½ cups water
½ cup pine nuts
2 Tb unsweetened carob power
2 Tb maple syrup
4 dates, pitted
1 tsp vanilla

Soak flaxseeds and dates in 1 cup water for 25 hours. Blend in a blender until smooth. Add remaining water and all other ingredients, blend until liquefied. Serve cold.

"Courage is not simply one of the virtues, but the form of every virtue at the testing point."
c.s. Lewis

Basic Nut Milk

1 pound raw nuts, shelled
Water to cover

Place nuts in a bowl, cover with2 inches of water. Cover bowl and soak for 24 hours. Drain nuts and rinse under cold water. Put half the nuts in blender and cover with about 2 inches of water, blend until very smooth, pour in another container and continue with rest of nuts. Pour all through a nut milk bag (find on eBay or Amazon) or cheese cloth. Squeeze all the liquid out of the bag. It should have the consistency of whole milk. Thin with a little water if desired. Will make 5 to 8 cups, depending on amount of water used in processing. Keep in refrigerator for 5 days.

Cooking Tip: no butter milk? Substitute with 1 tablespoon cider vinegar or lemon juice and enough milk to make 1 cup.

NUT MILK CREAM

1 pound raw nuts, shelled
Water

Same recipe as nut milk. After blending nuts,
pour through strainer to weed out any course
pieces. This eliminates nut or cheese cloth.
Makes about 6 cups. The cream should have
consistency of heavy cream. Keep in
refrigerator up to 5 days.
Cream will separate a little, just shake to mix
back together.

"You can learn a lot by watching."
Yogi Berra

Vegetable And Fruit Juice

Apple of choice
1 celery stalk
1 carrot
½ beet1
½ tsp lemon juice

Put lemon juice in container that the juice will run into. Thoroughly clean apple and celery, peel carrot and beet. Run through juicer. Run a little water through juicer if desired, better plain.

*"Let your food be your medicine
and your medicine your food."*
Hippocrates

JUICER PULP CHIPS

1 cup pulp from juicer
2 packets stevia
¼ tsp salt or to taste
¼ tsp lemon juice
Coconut oil

Mix pulp, stevia, salt and lemon juice, making a paste. Heat coconut oil on flat frying pan. Spread pulp paste in a thin layer and sauté until crisp. Alternative – oil cookie sheet and spread pulp past in thin layer and bake at 400 degrees until crisp. Break up into bite size chips and serve.

Cooking Tip: 1 tsp baking power. Substitute ½ tsp cream of tartar plus ¼ tsp baking soda.
1 cup broth, substitute 1 cup hot water plus 1 tsp bouillon or 1 bouillon cube.

COCONUT HOT CHOCOLATE

2 cups coconut drink
2 ounces bittersweet chocolate
Dash salt
1 tsp vanilla extract
Dash cayenne (optional),

Slowly simmer coconut drink, chocolate and salt, stirring to melt chocolate. Remove from heat and add vanilla.
Oh, go ahead and add a dash of cayenne. Just don't overdo it. Really picks up the taste of chocolate.

"You can be with nothing when you are not pleased with yourself."
Lady Montagu

SWEET GREEN SMOOTHIE

1½ cups almond milk, see recipe or if you insist commercial
1 larger frozen banana
2 ½ cups raw broccoli florets
1 tsp cinnamon
1 tsp honey or packet of stevia

Put all ingredients in a blender and blend until smooth

"It is better to conquer yourself than to win a thousand battles. Then the victory is yours. It cannot be taken from you, not by angels or by demons, heaven or hell."
Buddha

PINA COLADA SMOOTHIE

½ cup coconut milk, unsweetened
¼ cup plain whole-milk yogurt
½ cup fresh pineapple chunks
¾ tsp coconut extract
2 packets stevia or other sweetener
1 tsp lime juice
8 ice cubes
Garnish with lime slices if desired

Put all in a blender and blend until smooth.
Garnish with lime slices if desired.

"No knowledge is too much to bear in the end."
J. Brooke

STRAWBERRY-BANANA SMOOTHIE

1¼ cups plain whole-milk yogurt
½ cup silken tofu
1/3 cup no sugar strawberry jam
½ ripe banana
1/3 cup cold water
6 ice cubes
½ tsp banana extract (optional)

Put all ingredients in a blender and blend until smooth.

Cooking Tip: Tofu is a great source of protein, fiber and various vitamins. Put a little in: soups; nut milks; various deserts; puree silken tofu and use in smoothies, in lieu of mayonnaise, sour cream or cream cheese.

CHIA

1 slice fresh ginger
1 inch cinnamon stick or dash of cinnamon power
3 whole cardamom pods or dash cardamom power
2 whole cloves or dash clove power
6 black pepper corns or dash
2½ cups water
2 Tb sugar or 2 packets stevia
4 tsp loose black tea or 2 tea bags

Combine all ingredients except tea in a saucepan and bring to a boil, turn off heat, cover and let steep for 10 minutes. Uncover and bring back to boil, turn off heat and put loose tea or tea bag in mixture and steep for 5 or 6 minutes. If using loose tea strain into cups.

Cooking Tip: For 1 Tb cornstarch (for thickening), use 2 Tb all-purpose flour.
For 1 cup cracker crumbs, use 1 cup dry bread crumbs or panko.

ORANGE SMOOTHIE

1 quart vanilla yogurt frozen or ice cream,
softened
½ cup frozen orange juice concentrate, thawed
¼ cup milk
Orange slice for garnish it desired

Blend all ingredients in blender until smooth.
Scrape sides occasionally. Pour into glasses,
garnish with orange slices if desired.

*Holding on to anger is like grasping a hot coal
with intent of throwing it at someone else;
you are the one who gets burned.*
Buddha

STRAWBERRY SMOOTHIE

1 pint (2cups) strawberries
1 cup milk
2 containers strawberry yogurt (12 ounces total)

Keep 4 strawberries for garnish. Place remaining ingredients in blender and blend until thick and smooth, scraping sides occasionally. Pour into glasses, garnish with strawberries if desired.

Cooking Tip: To replace 1 cup cream or half and half. Mix 1 tablespoon melted butter plus enough whole milk to measure 1 cup.

LEMONADE

3 cups water
1 cup lemon juice or about 4 lemons
½ cup sugar or stevia to equal ½ cup sugar

Mix all ingredients until dissolved. Serve over ice.

SANGRIA

2/3 cup lemon juice
1/3 cup orange juice
¼ cup sugar or stevia to equal ¼ cup sugar
1 bottle dry red wine or nonalcoholic red wine
Lemon and or orange slices for garnish, if
desired

Mix first 3 ingredients together until sugar is
dissolved. Strain juices if desired. Stir in wine
and ice if desired. Garnish with lemon and
orange slices. Serve cold.

"Age is something that doesn't matter,
unless you're a cheese."
L. Bunuel

TEA VARITIES

½ gallon water
¾ cup sugar, better to forget the sugar, use
liquid and powered stevia to equal ¾ cup
sugar. More or less sweetener if desired
1 Tb lemon juice or to taste
Tea bag varities: 6 black tea bags; 5 black tea
with 1 bag peach tea; 5 green tea with1 or 2
raspberry tea; 5-6 raspberry tea bags; 5 black
tea with 1 mint; 5-6 mint tea bags; substitute
basil for mint; sassafras 1 Tb loose or small
root with 5 black or green tea; use any varity
of herb teas, plain or add 1 or 2 bags to black
or green tea. Mix it up have fun.

Bring 5 cups of water to boil, remove from
heat and put desired tea in water too steep for
a few hours. Mix into rest of water with
sweetener and lemon. Serve cold or hot.
Use loose tea or tea bags. Check out a health
food store for a big variety of loose teas.

"Get your facts first,
then you can distort them as you please."
Mark Twain

Sparkling Raspberry Tea

2 cups brewed tea (2 tea bags), chilled
2 cups raspberry or cranberry-raspberry juice,
chilled
2 cups sparkling water, chilled

Brew tea for 5 minutes, chill. Mix rest of
ingredients with chilled tea. Garnish with
raspberries, lemon slice and or mint leaf.

Apple-Banana Smoothie

1 Granny Smith apple, chopped
1 banana
1½ cup Greek yogurt
1 tsp cinnamon
5 walnuts
1 tsp chia seeds
1 cup ice cubes
½ cup water

Put all in a blender and blend until smooth.

*"To enjoy good health, to bring true happiness
to one's family, to bring peace to all, one must
first discipline and control one's own mind. If a
man can control his mind he can find the way
to Enlightenment, and all wisdom and virtue
will naturally come to him."*
Buddha

BERRY-SPINACH SMOOTHIE

1 cup frozen mixed berries
¾ cup plain whole milk yogurt
½ cup silken tofu
½ cup packed spinach
½ banana

Put all in blender and blend until smooth.

PEACH SMOOTHIE

8-9 frozen peach wedges
¾ cup whole milk yogurt or Greek yogurt
½ banana
2 Tb almond butter
1 Tb ground flaxseed (optional)
1 Tb chia seeds (optional)
½ tsp vanilla extract
¼ cup ice
¼ cup water

Put all in a blender and blend until smooth.

*"You can search throughout the entire universe
for someone who is more deserving of your
love and affection than you are yourself, and
that person is not to be found anywhere. You
yourself, as much as anybody in the entire
universe deserve your love and affection."*
Buddha

CITRUS PUNCH

1 can frozen pineapple-orange juice
concentrate, thawed
1 can frozen limeade concentrate, thawed
1 can frozen lemonade concentrate, thawed
3 cups cold water
2 quart lemon-lime seltzer water or lemon-line
soda

Mix all concentrates in punch bowl or other
large container. Before serving stir in seltzer
and or soda.

Make Ice Ring: use a ring mold or Bundt cake
pan, smaller than the bowl punch is in. If
desired slice about ¼ inch of lemon, orange or
limes, put on bottom of mold pour a little
water over and freeze when frozen add more
water and freeze. Run hot water over pan to
loosen ring, float ring in punch. Another idea
do the same with muffin pan.

Almond Coconut Shake

2/3 cup raw almonds
1/3 cup unsweetened coconut, shredded
1 ripe banana
1 Tb honey or sweetener of choice (agave, stevia, etc.)
½ tsp vanilla extract
¼ tsp almond extract
1½ cup cold water

Soak almonds overnight in water, drain. Mix water, sweetener, vanilla and almond extract in blender. Slowly blend in almonds, coconut and banana until smooth.

HOMEMADE PEANUT BUTTER

Place 2 cups dry-roasted shelled peanuts in blender. Add 1 tablespoon peanut oil and ½ tsp salt (omit salt if using salted peanuts). Blend 3 or 4 minutes until mixture thickens and is spreadable. Stop the blender and scrape sides if necessary. FOR chunky, stir in ½ cup chopped roasted peanuts after the blender is turned off. Usually have to stir before using.

Nut Banana Smoothie

1 cup of any of the nut milks or sunflower milk
1 banana

Blend all until smooth. Can't get easier.

I ♥ Tae Kwon Do

POSTSCRIPT

I sincerely hope everyone has found this book healthful and helpful.

Remember, recipes are a guide and you should feel free to add and subtract from them. As we know, at different ages our taste buds change from mild to a little spicier. Please take that into consideration when cooking for others.

Find out what you like and keep doing it, if it is healthy. Personally I have found the three day diet, at the beginning of this book, very helpful and I try to stay on it every week. Of course I like to tweak it every once in a while.

Good health is not something you are going to receive in one day, one week, one month or one year. It is a life time quest. Just like martial arts, it is an ongoing endeavor. Climbing the mountain can be very hard but when we get to the top we find coming down is just as hard.

As in eating and physical fitness the trick is pacing ourselves.

COOKING TIPS

To slice meat into thin strips for stir frying, partial freeze and it will slice easily.

For juicier hamburger add cold water to beef before grilling, about ½ cup to one pound of meat. DON'T OVER MIX.

Leave bone in for tastier meat. Plus bone in will carry heat inside quicker

When boiling corn, add sugar to the water instead of salt. Salt will toughen the corn.

To keep cauliflower white while cooking add a little milk to the water

To ripen tomatoes, put them in a brown paper bag in a dark pantry and they will ripen overnight.

Use greased large muffin tins as molds when baking stuffed green peppers.

To keep celery, scallions, asparagus and leeks crisp, stand up in water with a little salt and refrigerate.

Need to thicken something, try oatmeal or instant potatoes.

Few drops of lemon juice in the water will whiten boiled potatoes.

Want a little garlic taste in your salad, rub bowl with garlic before putting greens.

Over salted gravy? Put a little instant mashed potatoes. Add a little more liquid if needed.

Freezing fruit or other food that you want to keep separate in a single bag,
Spread them out on a cook sheet and freeze once frozen put them in a freezer bag and they will remain separate.

Whipping cream, put bowl in freezer for a few minutes before whipping.

LIQUID/DRY MEASURE EQUIVALENTS

<u>1 gallon</u>: 4 quarts; 8 pints; 16 cups; 128 ounces; 3.8 liters

<u>1 quart:</u> 2 pints; 4 cups; 32 ounces; .95 liters

<u>1 tablespoon / Tb</u>: 3 teaspoons/tsp; ½ fluid ounces; 15 milliliters

<u>1 pint;</u> 2 cups; 16 ounces; 480 milliliters

<u>1 cup:</u> 8 ounces; 240 milliliters

<u>¼ cup:</u> 4 tablespoons/Tb; 12 teaspoons/tsp; 2 ounces; 60 milliliter

HELPFUL IDEAS

Powdered sugar dissolves quickly and is best use for icings, meringues and cold liquids.

Tomatoes added to roasts will help tenderize them because tomatoes contain an acid that works well to break down meats.

Lemon juice rubbed on fish before cooking will enhance the flavor.

When tenderizing meat put in plastic bag to keep meat from splattering.

Need a great meat tenderizer, go to auto supply store and buy a plastic or rubber mallet. Works great.

Wet your hands in cold water before mixing or shaping ground meats. Meat won't stick to them.

Keep spices tasting fresh, keep in freezer or in a cool, dry place.

Per up the flavor of soup and stews by adding a few drops of lemon juice, red wine vinegar or a couple drops of bitters.

Put stock in ice cube tray and freeze, when needed just pop one out when needed.

The freshness of eggs can be tested by placing them in a large bowl or cold water; if they float, do not use them.

To make self-rising flour: 4 cups flour, 2 teaspoons salt and 2 tablespoons baking powder. Mix well and store in a tightly covered container.

WHEN IN DOUBT, THROW IT OUT.

LET'S TALK STEVIA

Just in the past several years commercial food chains have been offering different brands of stevia. South American Indians have been using stevia for hundreds of years. In the United States it could only be found in health food stores.

Leaves of the stevia plant are reported to be 15 times sweeter than canE sugar and the powered or liquid stevia may be 300 times sweeter than sugar.

Stevia can be an acquired taste. So don't give up on it. Try different types and amounts.

I like to use both liquid and powered together in my different recipes.

GREAT ADDITIONS!

- Maximo's Hot Sauce is a recipe from the U.S. Virgin Islands. It is a hot sauce that my family and friends have enjoyed for many years. We have decided to share it with you and yours because some things are just too good to be kept a secret. See www.cruzanhibiscus.com for details!
- Tabasco
- Celtic Sea Salt
- Himalayan Pink Salt
- Cayenne
- Black Pepper, ground and seeds
- Crushed Red Pepper
- Paprika
- Whole Oregano
- Thai Curry Paste
- Various other spices and seasonings

REFERENCES

Susan Silberstein, PhD "Hungry For Health", Infinity Publishing Inc., W Conshohocken, Pa 2005

Jeffrey Goettemoeller "Stevia Sweet Recipes", Square One Publishers, Garden City, NJ 1998

Elkins, Rita (1997) "Stevia; Nature's Sweetener", Pleasant Grove, UT: woodland Publishing

Richard, David (1996)" Stevia Rebaudiana: Nature's Sweet Secret', Ridgefield, Ct: Vital Health Publishing

Dr. Oz "Dr. Oz the Good Life", Hearst Communications Inc. NY, NY 2016

"Betty Crocker's cookbook Bridal edition", IDG Book Worldwide, Inc., Chicago, Ill.

Veronica Atkins, "Atkins for Life Low-Carb Cookbook", St. Martin's Press, NY, NY 2004

"Cuisine at Home", August Home Publishing Co., Des Moines, IA 50312

RECIPE INDEX

APPETIZERS & SNACKS

DESSERTS AND OTHER SWEETS

GREAT ADDITIONS!

MAIN COURSE

Nut Milks, Juices and Smoothies

SALADS and DRESSINGS

SOUPS AND STEWS

Made in the USA
Columbia, SC
27 June 2023

19499109R00104